This journal belongs to

_____

About this journal...

'What we suppress haunts us, what we express frees us'

There is a need in each of us to be heard and to express what we think and feel without censorship or fear of upsetting anyone. Love, joy, hate, anger, fear, confusion, doubt, desire, hopes, dreams, prayers and affirmations are all part of being human; they are valid aspects of who we are. The life force that flows through us is a river of creative energy that generates feelings, emotions and ideas which need to be expressed. If we try to suppress or control the flow, we become creatively and energetically blocked, and if the blockage continues for a significant amount of time it may also affect us physically.

Self-expression is healing. It is a natural and necessary part of leading a healthy, balanced and creative life. There are many ways in which you can express yourself safely without upsetting anyone. It is up to you to choose whatever feels comfortable. Drawing, writing, dancing, talking, screaming, painting, singing, running naked through a forest or your backyard at midnight are just some of the ways you can express yourself; the list is endless.

Expressing an idea can be the first step in making it a reality. Expressing a creative impulse can be a powerful unleashing of energy that can transform your life. Expressing the river of thoughts, ideas, impressions, feelings and emotions that constantly flows through us is vital. Where there is no flow, there is no life or vitality. Prayers can be answered, love can grow, anger can transform to love, healing can occur, clarity can be reached, peace and grace can descend upon us, magic can happen, when we express what is in our hearts and minds.

Expression is the planting of a seed that eventually flowers. This journal can be your flowering – it can be a place where you plant seeds of future creations; a place to collect your scattered thoughts, and express your heart's deepest desires or concerns. It can be a mirror that reflects your unique brilliance and the light and essence of your soul. It can also be a place where light is cast upon your shadow. There is possibly no safer way of expressing yourself than through this journal. There are no rules, except for this one: THIS JOURNAL IS FOR YOU AND ONLY YOU. It is important that you feel free to express what you want in any way you want.

Affirmations

The following affirmations are about your connection to this journal. They can be very helpful and powerful if you repeat them, perhaps on a daily basis for a while. I also encourage you to create your own.

Affirmations:

I will spontaneously express all I think, imagine and feel within these pages, without censorship or judgement, in any way I choose. I will honour, love and value everything I express in this journal in the knowing that all is, in essence, light pouring out from my heart.

*

This journal is my sanctuary, a place I go to relax and just be. There is no right or wrong here; there is only love pouring out of my soul. There is nothing about me that I need to fix or change; I love and accept every part of me as I am. There is an infinite ocean of creation inside me. The Universe is expressing endless love through me. There is vast space inside my heart, creative energy without beginning or end. I AM ALL THAT I AM. I am a particle of light, I am life, I am devoid of space and time, I am space and time, I am one with all, I am duality also.

*

These pages are a fertile field where I plant my imaginings, thoughts, hopes and dreams. They will be an exploration, a celebration, a meditation, a sacred journey. I am blessed by an outpouring of inner light which helps me see through illusion and perceived faults. I let go of judgement and the need to label things as good, bad, beautiful, ugly, right or wrong. I look within and see the perfection of life. Beyond all thought and suffering there is only love – a vast ocean of love.

Creativity

A thought on that which is beyond thought.

For many years, I held workshops on intuitive art and writing. The people who attended were of all ages and backgrounds. Many of them were initially very timid and seemed afraid of not measuring up to either their own or others' expectations. But their fears dissolved as they realised the workshop was not about performance or producing anything. I made it clear that the workshop had nothing to do with artistic or writing talent. It was not about techniques or formulas, it was simply about self-expression and self-discovery. The only requirement was to be open and not judge anything or anyone, especially themselves. I realised that when people feel safe, accepted and loved, the protective amour melts away and their inner essence shines through.

I discovered that everyone is creative, and everyone is a channel for creativity to flow through. Creativity is life force, and we all have it. It may sound strange, but I'm convinced that the major obstacle to creativity is thinking. Thinking and reasoning block the flow of creativity because, a bit like a computer, the mind, when engaged in thinking and reasoning, can only process pre-existing data – it can only drag up what has already been. Creativity, on the other hand, is a living energy; it is infinite, it is always from the unknown, always arriving for the very first time, fresh and new. It created everything we see around us. The greatest artists who ever lived did not possess any more creativity than you or I. They simply realised that creativity is an energy; a force greater than themselves, and they found ways of allowing that energy through with minimal interference.

You can learn how to draw, paint, write, dance, sing or play a musical instrument, but you cannot learn creativity. It is something you already are and have; all you need is to allow it through without prior analysis or thought. It is that simple, just allow it to be what it wants to be and not what you think it should be. Try it, practice this, and it will surprise you. You will discover that creativity is a wild, super-intelligent force with a heart and mind of its own. It doesn't need you to figure it out or think it into being. It doesn't need you to understand it, manipulate, master or control it. It just needs you to allow it. It has already created an infinite amount of things, like the universe, every form, colour and texture, so trust and let it show you the way – it does have a lot of experience in this area.

With love and blessings,

Toni

Look within. There is something beautiful, something sacred inside you — a space full of infinite wisdom.

*Feel it all around you, feel it inside you,
an infinite, all-embracing and creative field of love.*

*Every atom of my being is filled with
the same love that moves the earth and stars.*

I tune out of the noise and confusion of the world and tune in to a space of infinite peace and love within my heart.

*Love is always present.
My true nature is love.*

*There is no better time than now to go within.
There is no other time but now.*

*A powerful creative force flows through my heart, mind and thoughts.
I am one with all creation.*

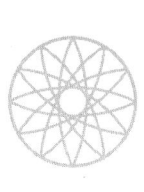

I rise above the transient thoughts of this world and enter a crystal clear space of light.

I am light.

*Creativity flows through me like a river.
I am a channel, an expression of its love.*

The Goddess of Creation dwells in my heart.

Eternity is a very long time, and yet no time at all.

Your spirit is ageless and timeless.
You are a timeless soul in a world of imaginary time.

*This breath, this moment,
this dream flowing through me is eternal.*

Beyond this mind that thinks about what to say and how to say it, is a higher mind that says everything without thinking or speaking.

Inside every atom, there is endless space.

I embrace you through the spirit of these words.
I embrace you through the spirit of love.

Divine Mother, forever present in my heart, renewing, destroying, building, transforming, blessing every moment.

Through the sound of the breeze
Through a whisper from a star
Through the spirit of the trees
Through a ray of sun
I feel you

Beyond the crashing waves of thought, there is an ocean of infinite peace.

*My soul is an ocean of light
reflecting the glow of an inner sun.*

The wisdom of trees guides me.

*Life is without beginning or end,
forever changing, forever unchanging.*

A tide of emotion ebbs and flows upon this page.

Just beyond the surface of this human drama, there is a space of infinite love.

*I am grateful for all that I am and all that is.
Blessed Be.*

I am the author, director and star of a most intriguing play — my life.

*In the silence of nature,
one can hear the song of the earth.*

Sunlight streams through trees, a gentle breeze blows, a leaf falls, and the earth smiles.

Dreams are the meeting point between the conscious and the unconscious, the merging of Heaven and Earth.

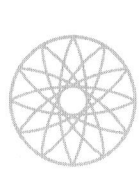

From within the heart of the earth, many future Earths shall be born; from within the heart of this life, many future lives.

*I feel an ocean of dreams, memory, feeling and emotion
flow across these pages.*

*Ask the wind a question
and be answered with a gentle breeze.*

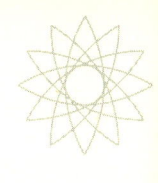

Every moment is one eternal moment.

A star glows inside me.

Calm the mind, and find yourself in another dimension.

I was once a particle of light. Now, I am a trillion stars.

I am spaceless. I am timeless.

I am grateful.

*Looking forward one million years, all has transformed to light.
I am a body of light, the earth is made of light, and all is one through light.*

*All I feel, I express without judgement or censorship —
the good, the bad and the ugly —
in the knowing that these are simply labels.
All deserve to be loved.*

Change is life's creative flow.

*The essence of creativity is love.
The secret to unlocking creativity is love.*

Today I honour life by expressing how I feel.

Today I honour life by doing something I love.

A stream of creativity flows from an ocean inside my soul.

I am a grain of sand on an infinite shore.

Today I accept and love both the positive and negative aspects of myself and others.

Today I love and accept the world as it is.

Today I remember that everything out there is also within me.

When the mind is not at war with the heart, there is peace.

The space between my thoughts is a gateway to infinite creation.

Creativity ebbs and flows in my heart.

When my dreams become a reality,
I remember it's all a dream.

Love is the only thing we take with us.

Sometimes obstacles are a blessing in disguise.

Creativity is the life force within everything.

Even a stone is creative because its every atom is full of life.

Creativity is a mystery that cannot be understood.
It can be erratic and wild or calm and full of infinite peace.
Creativity is life expressing itself through you.

Creativity is infinite.

A million years from now, the same light glows in my heart and the same love glows in my soul.

Love is the blessing.

*Today is the start of a new chapter
in the beautiful story of you.*

*Something inside you is glowing brighter.
Something is healing, shifting, unfolding, transforming.*

Express the inexpressible.
Release the uncontainable and untamed part of you.

Breathe in light — breathe out love

*This time will not come again
because it will never cease to be.*

The smallest thing can have great potential.

The power of the entire universe exists in each leaf of grass.

There is a universe within a universe within a universe within us.
There is awareness within awareness within awareness within us.
There is light within light within light within us.

I am changing as I write these words, and you are changing as you read them. Still, there is something inside us that is forever unchanging.

Life is infinite possibility.

Beyond thought, there is perfect peace.

What I focus on, I create.

Universal will moves the earth and stars.

*Today I listen to and follow my heart.
Today I listen to and follow the wisdom of my soul.*

*Positive and negative are soul mates.
One cannot be without the other.*

*Anything we try to change will not change
until we accept and love it.*

*Today I will keep an open heart and mind.
I will remember that a higher force is constantly at work in my life.
I will remember that I am safe and loved.*

All I need I will receive at the perfect time, in the most perfect way.

Only in being true to me can I be true to others.

I feel life blossoming inside my heart.

Today I shall not doubt. I will trust instead.

Within the light of love, there is unlimited creativity.

*Through a luminous event, we are born.
To a resplendent light, we return.*

Today I trust that all will work out for the highest good of all.

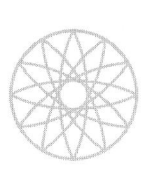

*Today I shall be a channel
for the light of my soul to flow through.*

*Today I will love and honour myself and others
by expressing how I truly feel.*

Today I will remember that I am an actor, playing a role that my soul has chosen.

This hour is part of eternity.

The happiness I seek is inside me.

*I may not have the power to change the world,
but I have the power to change my perceptions.*

This life is but a moment in eternity.

Today I allow my imagination to drift beyond the horizon of time.

Today I will reflect on all the beautiful memories of my life.

Today I will try my best to be fully present in each moment.

Today I will find the courage to be myself.

Through imagination, the invisible is made visible.

*Life is a tapestry where each stitch has a specific place and purpose.
Each is an integral part of the whole.*

Stars are born through explosions of love.

As the sun rises, may each heart give thanks.

Your soul doesn't care what you do or don't do. It just loves you.

Today I will plant a seed of love, a seed of kindness and a seed of compassion.

Every ending is a new beginning.

I give thanks for every blessing.

I imagine I am golden light. I imagine I am a violet flame.
I imagine I am a universe of colour.

Nothing is ever truly lost,
for all exists eternally in my heart.

Today, each time I have a negative or critical thought, I will consciously change that thought to love.

It takes no more effort to dream big than to dream small.

Today I will not stress.

*The universe is alive
and listening and responding.*

*If something doesn't feel right,
it's not right for me.*

*When you see beauty in another,
let it be a reminder of your own beauty.*

Only through darkness can we see the stars above us.

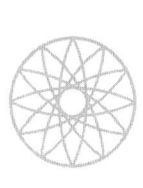

*Thoughts are living energies that hold enormous power.
Loving thoughts create loving experiences.*

Life is a deep well full of endless creativity, ideas and possibilities.

Love yourself unconditionally — every part of you, just as you are, without trying to change any part of yourself. Forget about who you could or should become and know that you are perfect just as you are at this moment.

Before you lies the path of new beginnings; an inward path that will lead you to discover the radiant being you truly are.

*Acknowledge what you feel in your heart.
No dream is too great within this cosmic dream of life.*

*Your creative power is equal to that of any artist, thinker or inventor.
All creativity is infinite and stems from the same deep well.*

*Plant seeds of love,
and a beautiful garden will grow in your heart.*

An autumn leaf falls into the arms of the Divine Mother.

*Beyond this reality,
there is a multidimensional reality
that is infinite and eternal.*

From a spaceless space, the river of life flows into the ocean of your soul.

In the physical world, all is impermanent.
In the spiritual world, it is eternal.

This world stems from a point within you where there is no distance or time, no coming or going, no losing or finding — there is only the eternal present.

Nothing is completely right or wrong.
Realising that life is full of contradiction is the first step to mastering it.

Through our darkest moments, we may come to see things more clearly. When we give in to life and no longer try to control it or make it happen, we find peace and clarity. Life and creativity start to flow again, and we hear that inner voice once more.

The light of your soul glows infinite wisdom, greater than all the knowing of this world.

Your soul seeks nothing or wants nothing. It simply loves you. At this very moment, its healing light fills and surrounds you, just as it fills and surrounds the earth and universe.

*Follow your own guidance.
Don't let your plans and dreams be crushed by the opinions of others.*

Each moment is a gift, each challenge a blessing

Without distinctions and opposites, nothing would be perceivable.
Would we know what light is if it were not for darkness?
Or know what love is if it were not for hate?

*When there is no contrast, we cannot distinguish.
Imagine living in a light-filled room without ever experiencing darkness —
you would not know either.
The fabric of creation is woven from complementary opposites.*

The fertile void of creation is a mystery yearning to be filled.
Darkness and light are intertwined. One is always flowing to the other.

*Live your life joyfully,
knowing that love always guides you*

*Ultimately, all of creation is one.
Division only exists in the mind.*

Through the eye of the soul, all is perfect.

Light and dark are aspects of you. Accept and love all you perceive to be good or bad about yourself. Love all equally and make no distinction between one or another, for all is a valuable part of you.

Connected to the present is an eternity.

Love does not separate, discriminate or judge.
It relies on us to do that and knows we do it very well.
Without separation, discrimination and judgement,
this amazing human drama would not be possible.

Let this world be a playground for your soul.

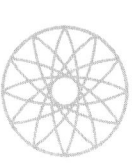

Life is the unfolding of divinity.

*If you need a mission, let it be to love the world.
This does not mean that you make no effort to help change things.
It simply means that you do everything you do lovingly.*

When people ask me where I get my inspiration from, I answer, "From life." Where else could it come from?

In the physical tree, there is the soul and spirit of the tree, immortal and eternal.

Every atom of existence is full of life and energy moving through space.

An atom of love melts into your heart.

This life is beyond understanding, words or description.
We exist, we are alive, we observe, we dream.

Your imagination is your creative centre.